# VOTIVES:

## ENTRIES FROM THE DAYBOOKS OF GERTRUDE TATE, 1898-1952

TRICIA YOST

Radial Books

Also by Tricia Yost
*First Things*

Copyright © 2017 by Tricia Yost
All rights reserved.

The poems in this book though they may reference historical events, real locations, and/or real people, are fictitious.

No part of this publication may be reproduced, distributed, or transmitted in any form or by any means, without the prior written permission of the publisher.

Published by Radial Books
radialbooks.com

Votives: Entries from the Daybooks of Gertrude Tate, 1898-1952 / Tricia Yost, 1st ed.

ISBN: 978-09984146-1-4

Book Layout © 2017 BookDesignTemplates.com

# ACKNOWLEDGMENTS

The poems in this book first appeared, in early drafts, in *Prairie Schooner, Ice-Floe, Syllogism, Smartish Pace, Lake Effect, Snake Nation, Art-Mag*, and *Hurricane Alice*, as well as in the chapbook, *First Things* (March Street Press, 2004). Grateful acknowledgment is made to the editors of these journals and March Street Press. Additional gratitude goes to Jill Osier, Kent Fielding, and Ryan Masters for their criticism in the shaping of these poems.

*Gertrude Tate lived with her intimate friend, Alice Austen, in the late 1800s, early 1900s. Given a camera at the age of eleven, Alice took over 1,000 photographs of life in Lower Manhattan and of her immediate surroundings on Staten Island. Her acute artistic and social sensibilities sealed her passion for the art form. Gertrude was a dance instructor and devoted companion. The two women lived together for over fifty years until a fire forced them apart.*

*<u>Votives</u> are selections from Gertrude's private daybooks.*

ENTRIES

MASKED, SHORT SKIRTS ........................................................... 1
THE LITTLE SHE HAS TOLD ME OF HER FATHER IS MUCH ..................................................................................... 3
IN SERVICE ................................................................................ 5
SONS OF ICARUS ....................................................................... 6
TO RECONSTRUCT SUMMER SKIES IN WINTER .............. 7
AT THE GATES .......................................................................... 8
A EXPLAINED IT THIS WAY .............................................. 10
FIRST AWAKENING .............................................................. 11
INVERTS, WE .......................................................................... 12
TO RECONSTRUCT A LIFE IS TO MOVE TO THE BREAKING POINT ................................................................. 16
A, AWAY, JUNE 1912 ........................................................... 17
BEAUTY CONSIDERED ........................................................ 18
PRECARIOUS, PROMETHEUS ............................................ 20
RETURN, EXHAUSTION ...................................................... 21
................................................................................................ 22
FIRST ACQUAINTANCE, HIGHLAND FLING .................. 23
RECONSTRUCTING HER MOTHER'S BREAKING ......... 24
LAMENT .................................................................................. 26
MASQUERADE ....................................................................... 27
SUN & DUST, MANHATTAN ............................................... 29
NOTES I ................................................................................... 31
WIDOW'S LIGHT ................................................................... 32

| | |
|---|---|
| HUMID, TANGLED | 34 |
| TARDY, MAY AFTERNOON | 36 |
| BOUNDARY WATERS | 37 |
| MOMENTS CARRY US THROUGH | 38 |
| MORE LIGHT | 46 |
| IN THE CITY, HARLEM | 48 |
| AT A LATE HOUR | 49 |
| ANOTHER EVE, ANOTHER YEAR | 50 |
| NOTES II | 54 |
| LINES TOWARD MAKING MEANING CLEAR | 55 |
| AFTERGLOW, JUNE 9th, 1952 | 56 |
| KINGDOM, SECRETS | 57 |
| ADDENDUM | 58 |
| VISIT TO A STUDIO | 59 |
| FEVER, A DIFFERENT FORM OF DARKNESS | 60 |
| IF IT DOES NOT BREAK US, LIGHT WILL LIFT US | 62 |
| WHISPERED AUBADE, ANY TIME | 64 |
| LONGING, AFTER ALL | 65 |
| CENTRAL PARK | 67 |
| ENTRY | 68 |
| I WILL ALWAYS BE GLAD THAT I FOLLOWED | 69 |

## MASKED, SHORT SKIRTS

In the bedroom
in petticoats,
matching Greek masks,
horse's hair past
shoulders, two
women smoke
cigarettes –
silhouette
all there is
to hide: the body –
urgency, held
by wig and
stance – by need,
her want, her
hand on my hip,
the other ashing a fag.
Touch is here,
symmetry not easy
to come by – she fits my
hands. Strong-
willed or jealous,
needy, calm, she
rotates forbidding
words and her fears

of what this is. She
battles a common
need for solitude, but
always returns to
the fit of our bodies.
She dresses
in costumes for the camera.
Masks her gaze.
Then after, she
drops her skirt, bares
her thunderous legs.

## THE LITTLE SHE HAS TOLD ME OF HER FATHER IS MUCH

She likes to think she has one memory of him:
the afternoon sun, the two of them in a rowboat,
his steadfast shoulders blocking the rays,
her small head seeking, hiding, seeking.

He has the day between ports, away from men,
furious seas, layovers in lands her mind doesn't
know to fathom. He knows only movement
and change. The cabin beneath the quarterdeck

is his only point of reference and refuge.
He spends the day off on water with her.
His rope-burned hands drag through gold
and spotted fins that rise with the lake's wide

ripples. His voice is deep and he is gentle.
She does not want the day to end. That day
that never began. Her playing mind seeks, hides,
seeks. That was not her father, but a friend's

father, the reverend from the church she and her mother
walked long and through scratchy woods to find. Her
friend was there, possibly her mother,
at a Sunday parish gathering of families, another

event where she tried to fill the missing pieces. Her father was thought to be in Holland, somewhere, elsewhere for certain. In this way he is not unlike God. She does not think of him often.

IN SERVICE

There are so few notions.
All white. All all. Beards and fists.
Limited in the one room
wooden A-frame at the end of the lane.

Simplicity is deceptive.
Inside dust motes are fairies.
Air hums between hymns.
We see once as children.

The sun tells stories though colored glass.
There's a man all elbows, knees, thorns, blood
Darkness everywhere

                then

When her hand grazes my hand
        sudden

                    possibility

## SONS OF ICARUS

There are stories of workers returning lightheaded,
dazed from the wind. We can see them, raised

ethereal forms, suddenly more than human.
More than what they were before they took the work.

The owners call it cast iron. Storefronts in Soho
are jailed behind its dark arms. Other uses

for those arms – Cathedrals of Commerce. Offices stacked
floor on ceiling on floor. Lexington Avenue,

Broadway. Building the city. The city. A journalist,
swings in a basket one thousand feet above

Fifth Avenue. He watches men in their shirtsleeves
and boots, pulling beams into place, securing rivets.

Tangled wires and cables hoist struts and machines higher,
still higher. A worker walks on parallel steel

supports. His wool cap, pulled tight around his scalp,
blocks the sun. Below, gray buildings hunker

on a grid of boulevards. The worker holds firmly
to the bowed alloy. He squints. He rises into the sky.

## TO RECONSTRUCT SUMMER SKIES IN WINTER

The sky is never to blame.
Summers end as they will
always. Loss
of splendor, birds absent
from eaves.

The sky is its own field
of color made full with the reflection
of souls. Fall soon, winter.
I fight a fullness that dares
my body combust.

Under the blue haze, I
remember movement. You
think: black, white.

In every season, our bodies
bring the world to us.

In every season, twirl
        rejoice.

## AT THE GATES

Uncle Peter mixes chemicals
in the cellar, dabbles in potions,
droplets, small explosions.

He makes a concoction
of calm for the wanderlust
child, tries to set her straight.

*You'll do better to marry*, he says.
She wants no bridegroom.
She is her own god. Mischievous

goat-girl, Daphne, fast
hunter, she flits and lolls about
the ground, ungrounded.

Heavy, underground heat.
Sweat from the lid of an eye
drips, plunks

into the mix. Peter tinkers
with this, that, keeps her
down with him.

He fears being shunned
for his spinster niece,
who is free with feelings

and fingers. Stepping
out of class, place,
she laughs at rigid faces.

Peter fears what she'll do –
stir too much, reverse
the earth's spin. She turns,

breaks beakers, runs
to the light – squints against
the white star. She leaves bricks

to crumble in Peter's damp cave.
Alchemist or witch
changing frogs

to women, she leaves
Peter in his cell
making coins for Charon.

## A EXPLAINED IT THIS WAY

*The nothing all around*
*doesn't feel*
*so full of nothing*
*when sunlight heaves*
*through the lens. Rough*
*      hot*
*        then cool,*
*fixed and resurrected*
*      in wet red bath, careful touch,*
*      drip dry.*
*  Memory made*
*      visible.*

*Palpable.*

*It does begin with light.*

*This is my language.*
*  This is I*
*    speaking*
*   you*

FIRST AWAKENING

The day always begins with light.
The ocean washes blue in front of you.
Behind, green rushes the cottage.
You live between these worlds. One
the future, the other,
the past. Seagulls cut endless lines in
the sky. From your perspective
there is nothing to do you haven't already
been doing. Daily you go finding
worth in every light. You know
this is all there is. You see
radiance, its speed and density.
You think finally to call this God.

## INVERTS, WE

The arch under the road bound the walls
on both sides for support. The ground
being stable, the women destroyed the walls
and leaned against each other.

~

A turning upside down inside out, as if one
were a sock, dirty or clean,
or a glass for water, half empty or full.
as if the self were not bound
in the body. Open the skin,
only blood.

~

Stratified rocks folding and folded over each other
and over bodies lunging and folding hiding revealing rolling

~

In meteorology, an atmospheric condition
in which the normal properties of layers of air
are reversed.
> I photograph Alice dancing.
> She takes my breath. I, hers.

~

Naturally, Eve falls in love with the woman in the pond.

~

An invert is phonetically sound.
Alice recites the alphabet on my vulva.

~

The temperature at which two forms can coexist in equilibrium.

~

Sex instincts turned in: in turning of instincts sexual. Much like stratified rock layering itself. Turning in to break out many hidden selves.

~

*The self*, Alice says, *is image, flipped and turned, shadowed and illumed, but never, never singular.*

~

In music, the recurrence of a theme, but in the opposite direction.
> Alice and I in full gown regalia.
> Sun dark – I kiss back.

~

Loving the neighbor as thyself
because the neighbor is thyself.

The pursuit of wholeness is love.
Theoretically, we can love anyone.

~

Not giving oneself to another but to oneself. The true nature of a mirror.

~

We go in to capture what is absent without. Turning and tuning in to the central mystery of the self.

~

On the lawn in men's clothing, Alice photographs herself.
She de-robes and photographs herself, too.

Alice: a separate self of many selves.

~

   Nerves tightrope taut
   deep breath and step soft
   toward Alice who turns
   toward me arms opened out

~

I turn in as if walking a hallway of successive, endless open
doors into a new century I turn in.

## TO RECONSTRUCT A LIFE IS TO MOVE TO THE BREAKING POINT

Every day was winter. Every day brought snow.
All that time wrapped in a blanket, by taper
her mother read hours into the night. She read
away the night. Snow filled the chimney.
The cottage became drafty. She did not notice.
This was her way of welcoming winter.

Neighbors say she swooned and opened flush
for the sailor. Neighbors say she danced
through the night because dawn was breaking
all through her body. They say they saw her
under the summer sun shed her stockings and gather
handfuls of her gown and wade into the dark water.
They say the captain she'd dreamed, dreamed along
the short edge of the earth, finally pulled all of her in.

Back then, snowdrifts bantered along the beach
like so many schoolgirls left to themselves.
Back then, ice crystals didn't hang like daggers
or steel bars. And then, at the door of the wood stove,
in her high-necked dress, she hid where she could not feel
the long ache of Indian summer.

A, AWAY, JUNE 1912

>Sleep comes hard
>without you. Touch me
>
>when you arrive. If I feel you,
>know I feel. Touch me –
>
>don't look past. My eyes
>strain in the dark.

## BEAUTY CONSIDERED

A woman on a fainting couch, her naked body draped
in a languorous pose. Whether real or imagined
there are needs surrounding the body bared.
The owner's need for cover, the artist's need to look,
everyone's need to be revealed.

Alice places the woman's elbow at hip's juncture.
I see her attachment to this nude who is an art
theory of balance and light. The body lying
before the lens. An ideal self, one of many.

Alice's normal eyes wander, wonder, fixed as they are
in wanting to disclose.

The woman turns her head slightly.
Hair crowds between her shoulder blades,
recoiling after pluming falsely.

When Alice looks later, memory's night
Between lovers confuses theory with form, form
with model, model with flesh, flesh and beauty.

Beauty which she tries to perfect another day
with the light descending through a window, cutting
shoulder to hip. A model of the Venus de Milo
in a constructed bed. Beauty, or the notion of beauty.

As if it were the flawless symmetrical slash
from the eye of an artist centuries dead.

The model gazes past the viewer. Her mouth
is closed. She has no hands. Her heart is alabaster.
Beautiful as Lavinia is beautiful: tragic.

Alice forbids nothing because nothing is
everywhere, is all we know.

New angles of the same body contorting
as she ties and unties a rope around the figure's hands,
tightens, loosens whalebone along the spine.

She dresses the woman in trousers because beauty
is never harmony, but what rises from a woman rendered
silent who speaks anyway, what rises from a woman
dressed in men's clothes, or from knowing that a man
could so readily be a woman, and that Venus is simply
a statue if seen from a distance.

## PRECARIOUS, PROMETHEUS

She pokes at the fire with the instinct to withdraw,
feels heat, but does not want my touch. In the fire
a glass flower disappears into flame. This is how we are:

easily shattered or vanished. Some nights on the veranda
she watches the sun set over the water, its blaze graphs
the screen. She feels wicker through her robe. She needs

these nights, sitting silent and solitary in the empty air.
Certain nights, she's a traitor, devising her own
Prometheus, daring, haunted, creating predators

out of nothing but safety, my fire. She digs with chewed
nails at her liver, her heart, which I mend over and again.
Set her free not with the strength of ten men but that

of a single woman. Tonight I kiss her shoulder and slip
from the covers to escape nightmares. Bare feet
in moist dirt, sinking, I breathe deeply

because my dreams leave me short of breath,
with the pain of a breastbone cracked. We are separate
until need draws us back.

## RETURN, EXHAUSTION

The sail of the ship is the dress
        billowing, blowing
back to harbor. After a breezy
tour, I return
to her rough, stiff docks.

..........

Poemmaking must be lonely
business. Tennyson in the tower,
Emily in the attic. The long, crowded
hours. A single, fickle candle.

Today, an organ grinder stooped by age
and the dissonant sounds of an instrument
ten years out of tune.

These moments of mine, scribbling
notes in this daybook, scoring moods,
making some sense of any event,
are lonely and long.

My body is exhausted after hours of dance
and walking the city with Alice. I've secured
this parchment to relieve the mind,
which seems never to exhaust.

Today, the rugged face of a thin woman
in a tattered frock selling apples in Manhattan.

So very little endures. This thought.
An afternoon performance.
A fragile page collecting
remnants, small records of a stunned life.

## FIRST ACQUAINTANCE, HIGHLAND FLING

Trees fill the windows with explosions
of green, fractured bands
of sun streak wood blond. Hair
wisps softly about my head
as I swing through the door, cutting
the fine-polished floor. If Alice knew
the hop, she'd take my hand,

catch the tail of my dress,
ripping clean the cotton. We'd
tumble against the phonograph,
and jostle music free. I
would help her to her feet, curtsy,
laugh, and commence a dance,
slow, seductive.

## RECONSTRUCTING HER MOTHER'S BREAKING

Sailor's barrel chest, large hands, dark silvering
hair. Eyes that reached into her. She must have
felt nothing but his need. Her need coming,
going. She was older and felt the sting less.
Complacency lodged in her bones, she had accepted
becoming old alone. He wanted to marry and wanted
her to leave her family. He must have wanted her dearly.
Indecision tapped with a metronome's hand.

Was it love or necessity?

After the ceremony, two weeks in the country.
His hands on her back at night.
Soft laughs, smiles, kisses. The reasons
for skin. Whispers of his travels.
Her body opening, a flower's ferocious bloom.

And then the city. Each day he brought her candies. She
made him toast and tea with sugar. When he slept late, she
wrote home of the house and weather.

And then the shortest of letters:
*Today marks two months. My news doesn't please him.*
*He leaves early and returns late. The house feels small, the air*
*heavy. When he's home, his hard eyes disappear behind*
*tobacco smoke. He doesn't talk of England or salty sea air.*
*He doesn't talk at all.*

Alice arrives and he departs. Her mother watches
for him from every window. Absent two weeks.
She relearns how it feels to be alone. The demands loss
makes. The dirty want of another.

He left no word. She was forced to return home
after a year's sabbatical. The family had plenty
and spoiled Alice. Her mother hated standing, hands out.
Her beggar's face worn with want.

Books and Sunday service. Complacency burrowed deeper.
Anger in her, fierce steam:

*I gave in blindly to fancy. To a strange man's empty words.*
*Before Oswald's eyes, I was*
*content to read and sing out my days. Now hidden*
*in the church, hymns surround me, but I cannot lose me. What*
*I have is this wanting and*
*a daughter who reminds me.*

## LAMENT

She hasn't seen the sun
for days. The apothecary is out
of magnesium powder. Candle-
flame is not enough.

With her tripod collapsed
in its box in the cellar, she thinks
this is what Adam must have felt before Eve,
then reconsiders –

what Eve felt after
seeing herself in the pond –
restless need. Women of slant,
they cannot bear not to act.

## MASQUERADE

We cut corset bone, pull it higher –
sucking me flat. *Too tight*, I gasp.
You loosen the knot.

Pantaloons billow wide, grandfather's
legs twice your size. His suit-coats,
Shirtsleeves drape you like a gown.

*Let's not go out, I look like a fool.*
You duck walk, Chaplin down the hall.
You bow, I curtsy. *Okay untie me.*

Moustache bristle tickles my lip.
You rip the hair, kiss me clean.
Undress me, loosen bone with teeth.

*Not now.* I quiver,
stepping back. You find
a skirt, hide your hips.

In the back of the closet, you dig out
smaller slacks, step in, don a coat.
You strangely gaze at the stranger in the mirror.

*We shouldn't*, I say. You laugh,
flame a cigar. You turn to dress,
cough, inhale again.

*They'll know*, I say, waving
aside the smoke. You shrug and fasten
my coat, then select a hat.

We step from the house into the sun,
*Are you sure?* I ask.
You bow, step aside, and open out my parasol.

## SUN & DUST, MANHATTAN

He slaps the rag
about her leathered foot,
spits and shines,
doesn't look up,
thanks her for the tip.

Vendors holler. Street cleaners
smack bristles against
the ground. We walk
arm in arm over cold concrete,
shop after shop. Bricks ladder
deep into the sky. She,
suited and proper,
leather soles, black mustache.
I, gowned and ruffled,
parasol open – inverted
tulip to block the sun.

We are bold but not so bold
in our clandestine strides. We pass
through crowds where workers'
rough hands wave us through, while
gentlemen tip their hats and women
smile. We laugh. Tip extra.
kiss in doorways and parks. Young
lovers to an unsuspecting world.

A ragpiler resting his barrel
grins hard at us. She tosses
him a nickel. With a flick
of the thumb, he sends it back,
picks up his wooden arms and pushes on.

Children dance around a woman
with roses, red and white. They
giggle when she places one
behind my ear. The woman
looks twice, feels the silver, walks on.

Down Fifth Avenue
in men's clothes, she hides
soft breasts and brown nipples
beneath a starched white shirt.
Wool slacks straight hide her hips.

## NOTES I

The mind is a field as open as the body
Sleeplessness is better when shared
There are no extensions except our own expansions
The Rosetta Stone is a woman's breast
There's only moving beyond our own likenesses,
   hardnesses
Skin makes demands that must be abided
We is never singular
Tender buttons, yes, drawers of tender buttons
Eagerness is an equation that equals heaven
There are endless lips and endless things to say
Closeness happens everywhere
Closeness happens here
Sadly, some people simply lack imagination
Existence is bare; we walk naked down the street
Woman and woman is not zero and zero
   but wholeness, loveliness
There is fullness and emptiness in even measure
Her breath winds us into each other
Unmapped worlds are far more interesting than
   mapped ones
The body decides with the mind
The soul offers pyramids of mirrors to a lightless
   world

## WIDOW'S LIGHT

Aunt Minn's sewing again
by signal light. She keeps
to her window through the night.

By telescope, she watches
ships ease through the Narrows.
Her mind narrows to foreign

ports, swinging times
with port wine
and her husband's shipmates.

She's the last of the family.
After Alice, the line breaks –
only females and photos. She

pokes at the piano, laughs
again at keys out of tune.
Her tone always a little

off. Deaf to what the world
wants. She's silent now
furled by the fulgor, waiting

for her ship. Alice's lips
are tight without a sign.
She sits by, book in lap,

keeping company as Aunt Minn
knits, no longer flitting about
the house in fun.

Her husband at sea
not to return, Minn's
dance done at 83.

She looks up, smiles
at her niece's eyes, ties another
knot of warmth. Alice looks

down and catches Minn's reflection
in the window where the candle burns,
almost out.

## HUMID, TANGLED

A tree cuts window's frame.
Sun slants over cobblestone.

Birds tangle in branches.
        Fingers disappear into hair.

~

Long undulations
Arcs of bodies

The sea plays rough
Against the beach.

~

Dark arc of spine
Over white sheets.
I lie in shadow
And wait for you
To enter.

~

Strike a match
The color of eyes
        Puckered nipples.

~

Song is the same as petaled skin,
Soft folds, dampness
       Rising.

~

Smoke circles
Battle at the ceiling

Alice stubs the cigarette.

~

Legs braid
   Lanolin skin
Spins toward sky,
   Spins
An arabesque of flowers.

## TARDY, MAY AFTERNOON

Burgundy crescent
on teacup's rim. Fingertip
breaks cool, oily sheen.

Cuckoo's ring echoes
off mahogany. Pushed back,
the chair opposite – empty.

Perfume lingers faintly.

## BOUNDARY WATERS

When we step out
of the house, water
cuffs our shins.

Rain. Many days'
worth. I've lost
count of the nights.

The harbor is spilling
into the cellar, which has become a shark
tank, its stairs a shoal.

Uncle Peter would cast a line.
Your mother would frown and wring
and wring her hands

at each ping of rain. Alice,
what shall we do? We're the ones
here. Everything is damp,

heavy with water. Will you make
our bed a boat, its canopy a sail
swelling toward crystal skies?

## MOMENTS CARRY US THROUGH

Through reeds and brush,
small hills, the Catskills,
she steps gingerly
on stones to cross a river.

I slip. She takes my arm, holds it –
locked triangles – the way home.

~

Alice opening out, pulling –
I follow with a smile.

Lush, rolling green. Laughing
water laps the shore.

~

Arcs of water captured in a square frame.
Light chisels sailors' shoulders.
Sails hold wind, force of daybreak – her
eye – so brilliant.

~

Arm in arm, Paris streets. Fountain's misty spray dances across A's arm.

~

With cigar smoke, wool slacks, twisted
black tie, thumbs snapping suspenders, she
fools the postman, a neighbor, but I
know the woman beneath the trousers.

~

With a tennis racquet for a banjo,
I sing and dance a larky life.
I wouldn't change a thing.

~

Summer in the Alps – taking a trail
on donkeys, legs dangling, slow
up hills, rocking, shifting
weight on the mule's muscles.

Alice straddles, *Giddy up*!

~

Alice hunched forward – 50 pounds
of camera weight. Later,

my hands on her back, kneading,
soothing.

~

Tango with Spanish men, sweat,
and heat. Tender pulses mark
hip turns. I laugh away
a hand's advance.

Alice absent from the floor.

~

Wet grass shoots between my toes.
I drag Alice to dance with me
in the thickening mud. My dirty
feet are so happy in the earth.

~

She marks me,
        over and over
old markings.

~

Cloud cover. Hailstorm. White
pellets. We dodge looks. Caged
animals too close. Cold
comfort in the unheated house.

~

Archipelago connections – lands dividing.
Wrong devotion! says my mother. Too old
for such nonsense. Her words bounce off the narrow
waters.

I leave her at the dock and greet
Alice on her island with open arms.

~

Figured satin, bouquet of violets.
Parasol out. Uniform bloomers. A cane's
tap matches my gait on the city streets.

~

Jacklight,
   moisture, tangled
      sheets.

The dog barks at rough play.

~

At the water pump cleaning her
plates, Alice is busy with the images.

At the window I watch
her reflection retreat,
I reach for her shoulder and
get trapped by glass.

~

Wet hair glued above her lip. Bristle
tickle against my thigh.

~

Smatterings of frost on the rolling
lawn. Alice steals
wet crystal's drift.

In the cold without a coat.

~

Gramophone's scratchy sound.
I mock dance because I'm alone on wooden floors.

~

Riding horses through Nebraska,
Alice says, *Cather's descriptions
are women's bodies.*
> *Making love.*

~

Dusty roads in a Model A.
Winds catch her scarf and reveal so much

skin I want to kiss.

~

A thousand nights of candelabra smoke limber.

Dipping toes in the Narrows, chilled,
Alice encloses me in her arms.

~

The kitchen catches fire and collapses.
Fire crawls out the door and paws at the garden.
In the storage room, Alice's images melt.

Flame chases me
back to the mainland,
Alice to a shelter.

~

Short visits. We sit close, hands
layered and light across our laps.

I want A's eye. I want her touch.

~

At water's edge,
Alice's body lets go.

A wheelchair in the sun.

## MORE LIGHT

She imagines she's blinded. Aperture closes black
around her, but she makes her way past objects – skims
the divan misses the buffet, moves through the foyer
toward the garden. Today it's humid. Sticky sweat

covers my skin. Metal clinks against dirt.
What I unearth she cannot fathom. What I bury
she won't know until spring. My moods haunt her
if she's open. Quiet patter on the carpet

or when feet hit hard, she knows not to speak.
If I twirl her hair, I'm lavish of heart. Because she can't see,
she thinks I don't see her. This is not true
I tell her with my touch. I'm grateful that she's still

for once, that she doesn't take the camera
when we go out. After a month, her muscles go slack.
She learns to crochet. Hooks roll between finger and yarn,
loop knot, pull tight. She learns silence.  She can tell me

what tree the bird is in, how high. She notes
exact timbres of my voice. In the morning
she picks tulips, in the evening I tell her they're daffodils.
Today, she bruised her thigh against a table I'd moved

and not told her. When I move I don't have to tell her.
At first touch my fingers are familiar.
Where does light go when it falls on blind eyes?
She remembers. It is enough.

## IN THE CITY, HARLEM

Hidden doorways hide clubs
in alleyways, smoky basement
bars. The low bellow of Bessie

mixes with the clink
of glass. Drag blues. Dark
men heavy with sound. The only

rule: anything goes. A witches'
brew of inverted looks. No
need to define nighttime

Harlem. Strangers and lovers
estranged cross paths, exchange
money, smile without pause

or second look. Lost in
the crowd, they find
a table, dodging Valentine's

Day circus, red hearts, red glow.
This district plays wild. Bessie
breaks, meets a woman offstage,

fools around. Two old women
drink their drinks, kiss
wantonly, this side of town.

## AT A LATE HOUR

After all the times I've wanted to put my tongue
in you, but could only touch your arm, after
your mouth cups my mouth, your hand
in the hair and lips between my legs, after
your body opens, closes around my hand, after
I give way to you, lunge and fold, after
honest fingers enter, enter again, after
our minds mix with the rollick of bodies, after
night gives way to morning and your mouth
on my breast circles the sun, after
I taste your wetness, after tenderness, after
I tunnel into you and horizons blur into lips, after
you give way to me, after fissures of light,
a cacophony of touch, still, this.

## ANOTHER EVE, ANOTHER YEAR

The century turns and I
turn with A.
It's been a year.
We'll plant flowers in the spring.

1900. What will the century bring?

~

Overcast today. No pictures.
Hunched forward, I pluck weeds.
I don't like too much glare.
A. fears the dark. Doesn't sleep at night.

She hopes it rains so I'll come in.

~

Suit and tie again.
We walked the streets.

Lost her mustache to the ferry winds.
I love the feel of her skin.
We kissed over waves on the way home.

~

In bed, sick.
Won't let her near. I fear it's typhoid again.

She refills the water when I sleep.
With cold cloth, wipes the sweat
from brow and cheek.

~

Fire in the Triangle Factory.
Three stories.
Smoke. Bodies burning.
Women jumping.
The women. The lives. The stories.

~

While visiting my sister,
the two Julias came
for pictures. The light
was right, A said. They romped
the island as men.

~

War an ocean away.
in drab gray-green form
she drives an ambulance with wounded
soldiers lying flat, careful to take
the snaking roads at slow speed.

~

The market crashed.
Don't know what to do.
Little money.
Just the house. Some photos.
Alice.

~

Fire in our kitchen.
Spread to the hills – the garden too.
There's nothing left.

50 years together.
Old ladies begin again.

~

We parted on garden's charred plots.
I took one trunk, a full life, rode
the ferry. Alice signed papers, took one last photo.

Rows of beds, musty air,
we stare at separate doors.

~

My last wish: to be buried
near the woman I have held dear
for many years. Bodies side by side.

Two markers to mark one life –
separate stones for this stolen life.

NOTES II

Regret is a stone lodged in the throat

There's a myth about forgiveness

Heroes are functional, but must be got around

The trick is to want what you've got

There's a grainy beauty to survival

What you let go doesn't come back

The sky will accept your blame

It is true that one can live a long time alone

There will always be light
There will always be dark

You could be sewing uniforms in a factory
that will soon burn

There are tender cities to be discovered

If I had it to do again
If I had to do it again
        Yes, I would say, Yes

## LINES TOWARD MAKING MEANING CLEAR

What we mean by sex, death, love is
the very blue of sky minutes after rain

a moth that draws to an exposed bulb,
the unfamiliar flame an equal, unavoidable lure

the golden laugh of a Nebraska field

sitting on the molding divan, a pug dog
on the floor, and rain, endless afternoons
of the softest rain

## AFTERGLOW, JUNE 9th, 1952

Arms slack from 80 years' weight.
Only the small of her back knows
the chair's plastic brace.

I wheel her over the grass.
Her hand on mine, her breath slow,
slower than wind's breeze. I say,
*Alice, let go.*
*Let go.*

Dry lips against my hand.
Lids close like aperture's mouth.
Last ships enter harbor for the night.
Only light is left.
Only light.

## KINGDOM, SECRETS

We're in the garden again. I'm her model, puppet.
After the shutter's close and opening, I walk
to the water's edge where rough currents
claw at the stable earth, where I breathe.

Later she tells me: *dawn was lacing the loose
locks of your hair. Your skirt swelled
from a brief wind and your feet left delicate
imprints in the unclipped lawn. It was perfection.*

I try to imagine, as Alice believes, that art is enough.
That her photographs of Galatea – no – of me, Gertrude,
are alive, pulsing. She must know it is not enough. There is
no color on glass, no movement.

Later she tells me: *light masks and ignites the self.
Endings and beginnings fold upon each other.
The sun goes right to my head.*

Later her eyes peered at me from behind a scrim.
She reached, withdrew. Hers is an art
of concealment and restraint.

I whispered: all that isn't movement is deadly. Listen, that's
the ocean. Its rhythms have planted
secrets in my body.

ADDENDUM

Shredded white across the sky
all that never was, is
only in the mind. Always only
tangled intentions.

## VISIT TO A STUDIO

He sells
one-cent a piece
portraits. Small,
wallet sized,
for children's
delight.

We'll be a Pickard
Penny Photo:
long tie, bow tie
the oddest hats we can find.
She'll stand behind,
hands on my shoulders,
faces with big grins, captured,
recognized by another lens.

Some think we're sisters or cousins.
Mr. Pickard sees the kiss and caress,
snaps away in his own glee,
takes his penny, hands us back:

two women poised, matted,
a life made just
small enough to carry.

FEVER, A DIFFERENT FORM OF DARKNESS

A black dog rummages in the garden.
A shadow falls over.
Alice brings a damp cloth to my inferno face.
Even here I'm aware she holds
her breath in the morning's muffled sounds,
though she tries not to as she tells me
the body's a fickle congress.

And tells I'm simplifying through typhoid,
burning out my father's blood, leaving his place,
replacing it with new shelter, callused hands.

Other parts, too, blister, burn.

She tells me I'm breaking down to make room,
that the things that don't kill us allow us
to carry more. She tells me
she has had enough of this sickness.
It's time to find a still point, pure
path unbroken, break-
water with her.

She's talking too much.
I'm walking a tight rope across Niagara.
Any minute I'll lose balance, drop deep and not rise.
My body is not my own,
tossed and thrown.

Alice is still
talking when the black dog
leaves. In the yard one single,
orange poppy. Alice breathes deeply,
above the cool surface
so do I.

## IF IT DOES NOT BREAK US, LIGHT WILL LIFT US

The sun shone over us while her lips curled
around syllables pouring from her mouth. I'd stopped
hearing sounds, and watched her serious face open
with new ideas. *Life comes at us without filters.*
*We cannot interpret without mediums.*
I was grateful for the day. *Hidden meanings*
*are made obvious. The angle is an act of will.*
I was thinking Aristophanes was mistaken.
Another won't make you whole. Alice, on her feet,
set the tripod. Caught rays bled gray into dust.
She couldn't salvage the plates I cracked,
in my anger, against the packed earth. Aggravated,
again, at her posing everyone, every little thing.
My sense of life is being in the moment,
being movement, moving despite song's end,
which never ends, only changes form.
Her moment is different – *the light – God's eyes,*
*when I believe in God – lifting me, the surest manifestation,*
*out of myself so fully myself.* She cannot bear
not to have that. This – the one solid thing,
this eye for the world. Water drowns, glass floats.
She must keep time – those fractions, compositions
for someone's eyes. What she brings into view:
the mark of women who've marked her. Whispers
against skin, night touches, honest fingers.
Simple stories shine from the shadows. If I knew
what she sees in eyes revealed by contrast, light

bent in the hands of interlocked fingers
or light as gift, clarity of curve, soothing gradation,
I would know, above all, it cannot break us.

## WHISPERED AUBADE, ANY TIME

Kiss and fold. Wrinkled sheets ruffled
over wrestling bodies.
I told her too much.

I sold my smile and then could not
speak. Fingers laced,
unlaced. My thoughts went cold.

Without – my body's left
blank. Nothing to hold. I
stare hard at light creeping beneath curtains.

## LONGING, AFTER ALL

Fire takes the house,
wood and furniture,
books, some
pictures. We
survive a forced
goodbye in the ashen
field that was
my garden.

I carry one
trunk, a full life,
board the ferry to the city,
back to dance classes,
crowded hours, men.

We lose. She
signs papers,
secures one last
plate – the burnt
skeleton. She
finds another
home, shelter
at least, with beggars,
organ grinders, others
who've lost
hold. Their worn
clothes match
worn faces.

Rows of beds
lined in musty air.
She keeps awake
to chopped sounds
of night breath, wide
echoings. She looks
toward the door and longs
for me to crawl
into her single bed,
for my hand on her back
to sing her to sleep,
rusty springs
to creak with the weight.

## CENTRAL PARK

Grass clipped short, trees
in full bloom, two women
in Central Park recline
toward one another

Cotton dresses
sleeveless and crisp

One smiles, the other
touches her arm

They see Alice, her camera,
move slightly
apart

Alice wants to say,
Don't move.
I know the ease
of hours of talk, the smooth
slope of a woman's spine,
afternoon's luster on pale skin

Or, move closer.
I know bird's flight
from formation, dew's slow
drop from young leaf,
thin weave near collarbone

ENTRY

After half a century, turn of centuries, Alice stumbles
through each day's unfiltered sky. She yearns for her
fingers to crack from fixer, an aperture's wide view, light
in her hands. I think of bare feet on bare wood, hard wood,
slap of skin or bare feet in the sand sinking in. Of petticoats
on Sunday mornings. Our linen snapping in the wind. Paris
hotel rooms we did not leave. Museums we did not enter.
The women's salon we did not bother to find. I watch her
arthritic hands scrabble through dusted plates.
Little endures. I once thought of our words as oak.
There are so many shadows. Things undone. Death,
separation, now, means nothing. Is everything. As if
fifty years were enough to know someone else's rhythms.
As if there were no limits. As if anyone can save you
from yourself. After this much time, I can tell you
there is a space between words and kisses. There will be
tiny openings. Seeing your veiled self in a photograph
is something like finding God. Most of your questions will
remain unanswered. If you move, you will find
the possible is an open field that pushes out to a cliff
where you can swan dive into cool, still waters.
You cannot rest, but must walk into the frenzy of first light.
If you're blessed you will find her and she will lace
the notches in your spine. Your back would have to break
to set her free.

## I WILL ALWAYS BE GLAD THAT I FOLLOWED

Alice picks my kerchief from the floor.
*You dropped this, Miss.*
Eyes refuse to shy away.
*Thank you.* My hand reaches
past silk, grazes her skin.
subtle shock, faint blush

*You're a wonderful dancer.*
*If I only had children*
*for you to teach.*

*No children?*

*No husband.*

~

Clouds clear as we approach
the riverbank. *Follow me,*
she says, bunching her skirt,
walking across water.

And I do.

www.ingramcontent.com/pod-product-compliance
Lightning Source LLC
Chambersburg PA
CBHW020624300426
44113CB00007B/767